First published 1980 by
Octopus Books Limited
59 Grosvenor Street
London W1

Reprinted 1982

© 1980 Octopus Books Limited

ISBN 0 7064 1359 8

Produced by Mandarin Publishers Limited
22a Westland Road, Quarry Bay, Hong Kong

Printed in Hong Kong

Educational and Series advisor Felicia Law

First Words

illustrated by
David Mostyn

The Attic

feather

skis

telescope

dollhouse

doll

key

cobweb

spider

toboggan

hat

rocking horse

album

trunk

7

The Zoo

zebra

kangaroo

cheetah

chimpanzee

peacock

giraffe

penguin

camel

lion

tiger

alligator

elephant

bear

apron

tap

sink

freezer

chair

cupboard

cat

recipe

refrigerator

The Kitchen

tile

saucepan

stove

mug

cup

iron

washing machine

ironing board

The Circus

tent

balloon

fire-eater

juggler

clown

The Supermarket

candy

cash register

counter

milk

sausage

meat

basket

The Park

pigeon

tree

greenhouse

orchard

ash can

dog

picnic

pool

squirrel

acorn

ant

flower

16

kite

oak

apple

bonfire

wheelbarrow

pushchair

spade

rake

lawn mower

swan

duck

rose

petal

17

The Marina

The Toyshop

jigsaw puzzle

teaset

cowboy

rag doll

parcel

baby carriage

record player

puppet

frisbee

records

soldier

counter

skateboard

lifeguard

snorkel

swimsuit

foot

hair

armband

float

22

The Swimming Pool

window

tile

body

mouth

water

nose

hand

23

The Football Match

player

shorts

whistle

referee

goalpost

goalkeeper

camera

football

photographer

scarf

satellite

control tower

helmet

astronaut

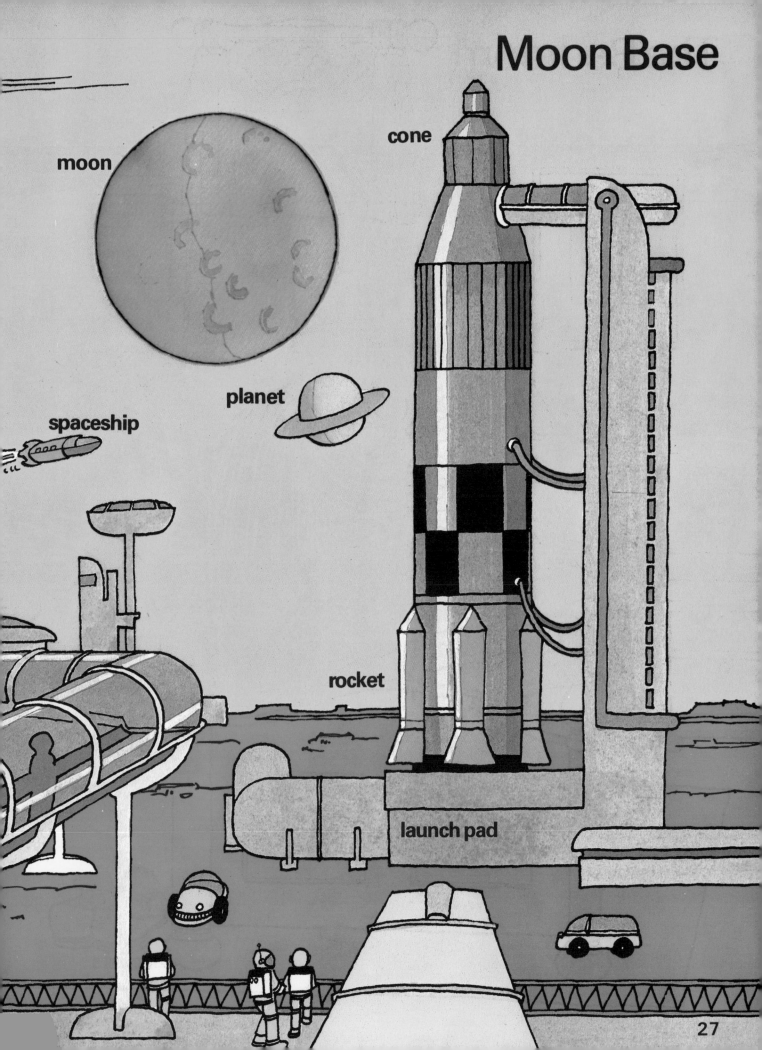

Moon Base

moon

cone

planet

spaceship

rocket

launch pad

27

The Bedroom

curtains

mirror

picture

toy

pillow

carpet

slippers

blanket

lamp

dress

bathrobe

bed

socks

shoes

The Workshop

wire

torch

spring

ladder

paint

wood

pliers

ruler

saw

nails

hammer

drill

sawdust

31

railing

jeans

merry-go-round

slide

pocket

32

The Playground

puddle

umbrella

swings

jungle gym

seesaw

seagull

sandals

flag

bucket

deck chair

sand castle

crab

seaweed

The Beach

ferry

goggles

skin diver

fisherman

pier

flippers

net

shell

pebble

35

blood

thermometer

patient

bandage

ointment

towel

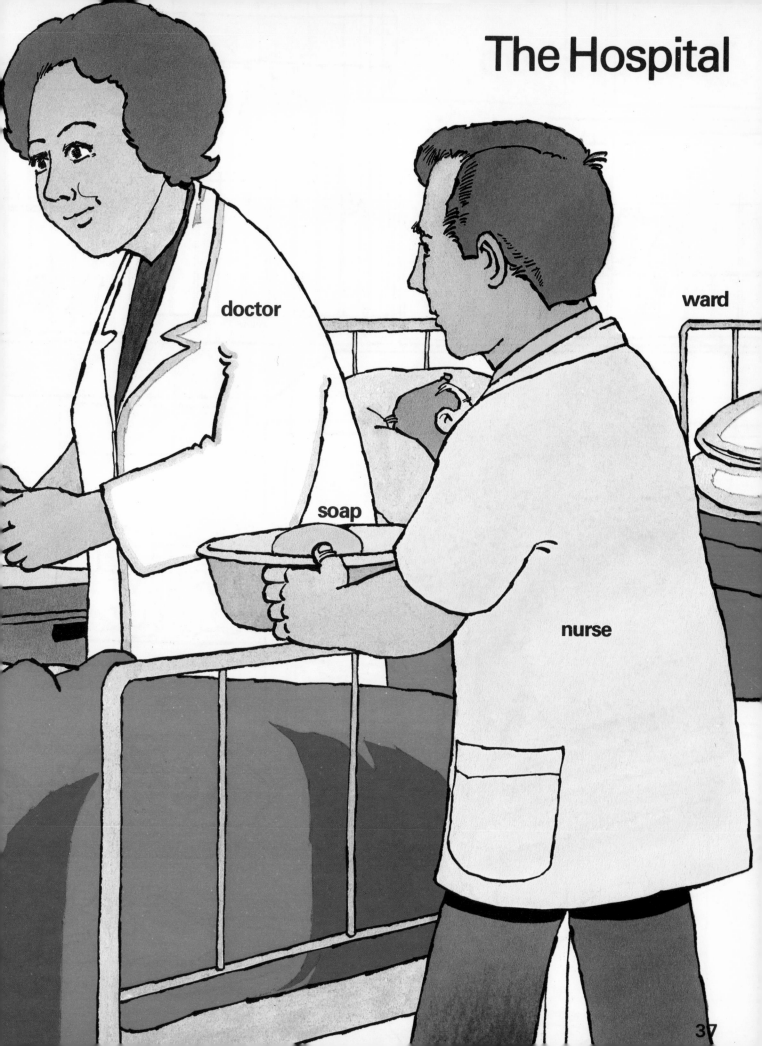

The Hospital

doctor

ward

soap

nurse

37

The Pet Shop

bird

hutch

kitten

puppy

rabbit

sacks

38

The Restaurant

waitress

glasses

plat

ABCDEFGHIJKL
MNOPQRSTUVW
XYZ abcdefghijklmn
opqrstuvwxyz

alphabet

ribbon

book

clay

table

42

The Classroom

teacher

pattern

scissors

paste

pencil

painting

paper

43

The Farmyard

field

gate

fence

farmer

pond

pig

straw

45